Thurgood Marshall

Supreme Court Justice

Written by Garnet Nelson Jackson
Illustrated by Higgins Bond

MODERN CURRIC

Program Reviewers

Leila Eames, Coordinator of Instruction,
Chapter 1
New Orleans Public Schools
New Orleans, Louisiana

Stephanie Mahan, Teacher
Bethune Elementary School
San Diego, California

Thomasina M. Portis, Director
Multicultural/Values Education
District of Columbia
Public Schools
Washington, D.C.

ISBN 0-8136-5243-X (Paperback)   0-8136-5237-5 (Reinforced Binding)
Printed in the United States of America

12 13 14 15   07 06 05 04 03

Pearson Learning Group

1-800-321-3106
www.pearsonlearning.com

Dear Readers,

As a young boy, Thurgood Marshall realized that he could speak well. When he grew up, he made good use of this skill.

As a lawyer and then a judge, he helped poor African American people win their cases in the courts of law.

Read to find out the many ways Thurgood used his gift of speaking to change unfair laws and to help all Americans.

Like Thurgood, we too should speak out to stop unfairness.

Your friend,

Garnet Jackson

"Thurgood, not again!" the teacher said. It seemed that Thurgood Marshall was smart but was always getting into mischief.

Almost every day Thurgood was in trouble. Almost every day he got this punishment.

"Go to the basement, young man. Read a part of the Constitution of the United States. And don't come back until you can say it from memory!"

By the time Thurgood finished school, he knew the Constitution by heart.

Thurgood's great-grandfather was from
the Congo in Africa. He was brought to
America to work as a slave. But he was
so proud and strong-willed that his
owner could not make him obey.
Finally he was set free.

Thurgood's mother, Norma, was a teacher at his school. She often talked to her son about misbehaving. But Thurgood, like his grandfather, had a mind of his own.

Thurgood's father, Will, had always taught Thurgood and Aubrey to speak up for themselves. On many evenings at their home in Baltimore, Maryland, Will would sit with his boys to talk. He taught his sons to give reasons and proof for everything they said.

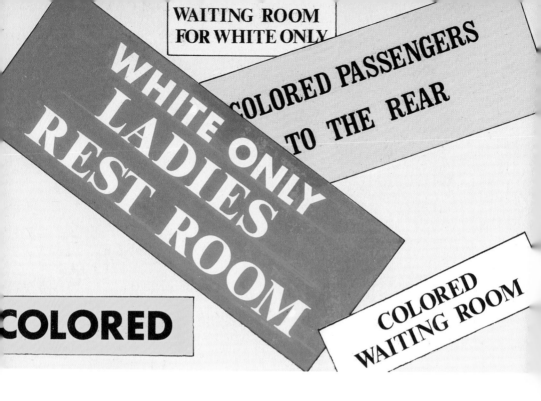

Sometimes Thurgood talked with
his father about the Constitution. It
promised equal rights to all people.
But what about African Americans?
Will Marshall knew that, fifty years
after slavery had ended, African
Americans still did not have
equal rights.

This idea stayed in Thurgood's mind. Thurgood believed that African Americans needed someone to help them get equal rights promised by the laws of the Constitution.

Thurgood started college at Lincoln University in 1925. He planned to become a dentist.

While at college, Thurgood joined the debating team. Because he stated his opinions and reasons well, his team almost always won.

Thurgood realized how much he liked winning an argument. So he decided to become a lawyer. He would argue for the rights of African Americans.

In college, Thurgood fell in love with Vivian Burey, nicknamed Buster. The two students married in 1928. During his last year in college, Thurgood studied harder than ever.

After Thurgood graduated, he began law school and held a job too. His days and nights were filled with work and study. When he graduated from Howard University Law School in 1933, Thurgood was one of the top students in his class.

Thurgood then opened a law office in Baltimore and helped many African Americans. He became known as the poor people's lawyer. Many of the people he worked for did not have money to pay him, but Thurgood helped them anyway.

The National Association for the
Advancement of Colored People—the
NAACP—asked Thurgood to work for it.
Soon he was the group's chief lawyer. He
traveled all over the country to argue for
the rights of African Americans. He won
many important court cases.

We the People of the United States, in Order to form a more perfect Union, establish insure domestic Tranquility, provide for the common defence, promote the general Welfare, and secure the Blessings of Liberty

Article. I.

Section 1. All legislative Powers herein granted shall be vested in a Congress of United States, which of Representatives.

Section 2. The House of Representatives shall be composed of Members chosen every second Year by the People of in each State shall have the Qualifications requisite for Electors of the most numerous Branch of the State Legisl No Person shall be a Representative who shall not have attained to the

Thurgood's most famous case was against the school board of Topeka, Kansas. In Topeka, laws said that whites and African Americans had to go to separate schools. Thurgood fought against those laws and won.

In 1954, Thurgood spoke to the Supreme Court, the highest court in the land. He proved that African American and white children should be able to go to the same schools in every state.

The next year, Thurgood's wife, Buster, died. Later he met Cecilia Suyat, whom he married. They had two sons.

Thurgood never stopped helping people. He led the way for many African Americans in the struggle for equal rights.

In 1967, Thurgood accepted his greatest job of all. President Lyndon Johnson asked him to be a judge on the Supreme Court.

21

About the Author

Garnet Jackson was born and raised in New Orleans, Louisiana. She is now an elementary school teacher in Flint, Michigan, with a deep concern for developing a positive self-image in young African American students. After an unsuccessful search for materials on famous African Americans written for early readers, Ms. Jackson produced a series of biographies herself. She has now written a second series. Besides being a teacher, Ms. Jackson is a poet and a newspaper columnist. She dedicates this book with love to her son Damon.

About the Illustrator

Higgins Bond was born and raised in Little Rock, Arkansas, and earned a Bachelor of Fine Arts degree at Memphis College of Arts. She has worked for almost 20 years as a freelance illustrator for such companies as the Bradford Exchange, and has illustrated three U.S. postal stamps. In *Thurgood Marshall*, she has used acrylics in a highly detailed photorealistic style.

Thurgood Marshall served on the Supreme Court until 1991. He died in 1993. He gave his decision on many, many cases. Each time, he remembered what he had learned as a boy. He tried to make sure everyone had the rights promised by the Constitution.

Glossary

Congo (käṇg′ gō) A country in Africa

Constitution (kän′ stə too′ shən) The highest law in the United States

court (kôrt) A group of judges, or the room in which the judges meet

debate (di bāt′) A contest in which two teams take opposite sides of a question; each team uses reason and proofs to try to show its side is correct

judge (juj) A person who hears a law case and decides which side is right

lawyer (lô′ yər) One trained in the law, who helps others in problems with the law